The Ultimate Guide
for Men to Understand
WOMEN

By Alex and Elizabeth Lluch

WS Publishing Group

San Diego, California

The Ultimate Guide
for Men & Women to
Understand Each Other

The Ultimate Guide for Men to Understand Women

By Alex and Elizabeth Lluch
Published by WS Publishing Group
San Diego, California 92119
Copyright © 2010 by WS Publishing Group

Designed by WS Publishing Group:
David Defenbaugh, Sarah Jang

Image Credit: Sandals: © iStockphoto/Skip ODonnell

For Inquiries:
Log on to www.WSPublishingGroup.com
E-mail info@WSPublishingGroup.com

ISBN: 978-1-934386-86-6
This book is part of a two-book set.
Not to be sold separately

Printed in China

Table of Contents

Table of Contents

Introduction

On January 20, 1974, American feminist, activist, and author Betty Friedan said to a crowd gathered in New York City, "If divorce has increased by one thousand percent, don't blame the women's movement. Blame the obsolete sex roles on which our marriages were based."

By the time Friedan gave this speech, the National Organization of Women (NOW) had seen an explosive increase in membership—from 1,200 to more than 48,000 in just a few years. In the midst of the expanding women's liberation movement, Friedan spoke to a crowd comprised mostly of women who were hungry to redefine the gender roles within their marriages—roles that men and women continue to struggle with today.

Confusion over gender roles significantly impacts how modern men and women relate to each other as partners. Indeed, as women struggle to balance their sense of self with their commitments in marriage and motherhood, men are often baffled at how to meet their partner's needs. Navigating relationships without clearly defined provinces, in other words, has led to a new front in the war between the sexes: the battle to understand each other.

Fighting to Understand Each Other

Without defined gender models to guide them, men in relationships are often left to flounder in confusion. Attempts to maintain a sense of manhood while being supportive boyfriends, husbands, and fathers can turn awkward—and be easily misinterpreted by women.

For example, most men are supportive of their partner's career, yet they prefer to remain the primary breadwinner. Thus, husbands say, "Congratulations!" after their wives receive raises and promotions, but may become sullen or short-tempered out of jealousy.

Likewise, men view verbal accolades as being supportive enough, while women long for further affirmation through demonstration of an overtly supportive attitude. Because women rarely feel their efforts are respected or appreciated, they get frustrated and over time come to resent their partners. Men, on the other hand, are left to wonder what they did wrong and how they can avoid confrontation next time.

Not being able to easily understand one another is a common problem and one that leads to much tension. A 2009 survey conducted by OnePoll estimates that couples spend about 10 days a year not speaking to each other as a result of arguments. Most respondents admitted that fights usually ensued as a result of comments that one partner viewed as insensitive or critical. Heightened sensitivity about who works harder, earns or spends more money, or takes better care of the kids and home are the top reasons couples fight, while pride prevents partners from making up right away. All such episodes stem from men and women feeling severely misunderstood by their partners. Men face a particular challenge as they try to navigate women who seem to constantly change their minds about what they need without clueing their men in. As a result, men feel like nothing they do or say is ever good enough, and even get sick of trying to figure it out after a while.

While there is no one method for understanding your wife or girlfriend, a good place to look for clues is in television programs, which have impressive influence over how people—and particularly women—view gender, sex, and marriage. According to TV-Free America, more than 99 percent of American households have at least one television and the average viewer will spend 9 years out of a 65-year lifespan watching TV. With so much exposure, and with so many programs devoted to the subject of relationships, television greatly influences what women expect their careers, relationships, sex lives, and marriages to look like.

Watch and Learn

To get an idea of where your partner's ideas about

relationships come from, watch some of her favorite TV shows. It is likely you will quickly recognize—and even be able to deconstruct—your partner's behavior just by watching the programs that have helped her create her ideas about relationships. Most women's relationship expectations are set impossibly high by the programs they watch and by the characters they most closely identify with.

For example, reality dating shows such as *The Bachelorette*, *Who Wants to Marry a Millionaire*, *Next*, *Temptation Island*, and *A Shot at Love* have cultivated an impossibly romantic yet cut-throat image of how to find (and keep) a partner. They send the mixed message that everyone has a soul mate—unless, of course, someone better comes along. Women who are devoted to these shows can't help but internalize some of the messages they espouse. Reality dating shows are almost diabolically structured to capture the attention and imagination of its primarily female audience members. They target women's deepest insecurities and wildest romantic fantasies as they feature droves of attractive, interesting, and rich men who vie for the affection of one highly desired woman. Lovestruck guys engage in macho competitions, humiliate themselves, pour their hearts out on camera, and even cry to prove their undying love. In comparison, the average marriage can seem boring and unsatisfying to a woman who deep down wants to be adored and pursued.

Women who watch these shows regularly are led to wonder what their husbands are willing to do to prove their love. Hence, just as many men suspect, their partners test them by asking so-called no-win questions such as, "What are you thinking about right now?" She of course wants to hear, "I'm thinking about how much I love and adore you!" Your partner actually believes there is a chance that will be your answer, because the television shows she watches inform her ideas about what love should look and sound like. In other words, she asks you that question because she makes the semi-illogical leap that since you love her, you must be thinking about her. After all, the men on her favorite programs do nothing but think about their potential soulmate. So when you answer "steak" instead of "you," her expectations are dashed and you have failed her test. Learning to recognize such tests—as well as how to pass them—is crucial for getting along with your partner. Ironically, once you learn how to successfully pass her tests, she will tire of testing you.

Other clues about your partner's expectations regarding gender identity, sex, and love are found in the popular HBO series, *Sex and the City*. This historically influential show analyzed relationships down to their tiniest details. It encouraged women to embrace a feeling of power in relationships and also advocated the idea that women are entitled to "have it all"—even when that "all" isn't very realistic. For instance, the show gave women the improbable notion that every single woman in her 30s could live in a fabulous New York City apartment, drink and dine at the finest restaurants every weekend, date wealthy and powerful men at every turn, and splurge weekly on designer clothes and shoes.

Women became so influenced by the show that it

caused them to wonder whether they had settled instead of striving for a more exciting lifestyle and fulfilling relationship. They wondered whether they could be having hotter sex, get taken to better restaurants, date a better conversationalist, or even be better off simply in a relationship with themselves. The show's characters were so iconic that millions of *Sex and the City* fans learned to describe themselves as a "Carrie," "Samantha," "Charlotte," or "Miranda," each of whom represented a relationship "type." Carrie cherishes commitment and needs her partner to demonstrate his commitment through his actions; Samantha requires passion and a fulfilling sex life; Charlotte always puts her family first, and expects the same from her mate; and Miranda seeks to preserve her sense of self by balancing career and family.

But most women, of course, are some combination of all of the above, and rarely are relationships as debonair, funny, sweet, or hot as the show portrayed them. What men must understand about women is that, like these characters and the women who worship them, female relationship psychology is always more complex than any one issue, and often highly influenced by storylines that direct them toward dating and marriage perfection.

Everything Matters

But even if a bit unrealistic, *Sex and the City* and other shows aimed at female audiences have helped women understand a universal truth about relationships— that all of their components are intimately connected. Modern women really believe that all issues between couples are interrelated and that everything you say and do matters. They see loyalty, commitment, fidelity, communication, priorities, values, sex, intimacy, finances, appearance, and health as related components of you and your partner's overall connection that require constant maintenance and negotiation. On this point, your partner is probably on to something. At the very least, recognizing the interconnectedness of the aspects of your relationship will get you closer to understanding what drives her to think, act, and react.

The Ultimate Guide for Men to Understand Women,

will help you unravel your partner's complexities by providing straightforward scenarios with well-researched advice for how to peel back her emotional layers and find out what's really going on. By employing the techniques outlined in each of the six chapters you will come closer to understanding not only your girlfriend or wife, but all of the women in your life.

Commitment & Fidelity

The days of commitment-phobia falling along gender lines are over: men are no longer unique in their fear of making a long-term commitment to their partner.

According to the U.S. Census Bureau, single women are the fastest-growing segment of the American population. Indeed, more than 47 million women—22 million of whom are between the ages of 25 and 44—are choosing to stay single. *Kiss and Run* author Elina Furman suggests that these women want to commit—they are just terrified of what they will lose along the way. Now more than ever, it seems, men and women can relate to each other on the problem of how to commit without giving up individuality.

One issue that prevents the harmonious pairing of two like-minded yet independent singles is that women don't quite know how to communicate loyalty in a way that men can understand. For example, men in relationships operate under the assumption that everything is fine until they are told—or shown—otherwise. They use physical connection, behavior, and action to judge whether the relationship is working. Women, on the other hand, are constantly evaluating their own happiness—sometimes on a daily, even hourly, basis. They prefer to talk about feelings as they arise, rather than developing feelings in reaction to a situation. In addition, women prefer to discuss their level of commitment and are likely to express their loyalty verbally, rather than through their actions. With such different relationship styles, it is no wonder men are so confused!

Figure out why she does what she does:

1. As Erica Jong once wrote, "Jealousy is all the fun you think they had." She is jealous because she thinks you are hiding something. Make the decision to be an open book and avoid secrets.

2. She needs to be reassured of your love through your actions and your words.

3. She judges your level of commitment by how invested you are in your home life.

down into components. For example, commitment can be demonstrated through loyalty, fidelity, participation in household duties, taking initiative in the romance department, or by giving up certain behaviors and activities. Once you break down your understanding of commitment, ask your partner to rank them in order of importance. Understanding how she views loyalty and commitment will clarify why issues such as jealousy crop up in your relationship—and prevent your partner from joining the ever-growing pool of women who are single-by-choice.

Tell Her You Love Her

Women need to be reassured of your love. When she tells you that she loves you, she expects you to say it back.

The Scenario

Your wife or girlfriend always says "I love you" before hanging up the phone, leaving for work and taking a trip—but you don't. You don't understand why this bothers her, because you think it's obvious that you feel the same way. Learn how to comfortably make small efforts that show and tell her you love her.

Situation at a Glance

- She frequently expresses her love for you verbally and wants you to do the same.
- You don't think it's necessary to say "I love you."
- She thinks because you don't say it, you don't feel it.
- You believe that actions speak louder than words, and that your actions scream, "I love you!"
- She interprets your resistance to saying "I love you" as a sign that something is wrong in the relationship.

- You wish she would stop obsessing over this small detail and pay attention to the ways in which you show her you care.

The problem in this situation

Relationship expert Dr. Deborah Tannen discovered in her research on men, women, and communication that men "use talk to preserve independence" while women, "use conversation to negotiate closeness and intimacy." This disconnect plays out every time your wife says "I love you," and you don't say it back. Clearly, you both have different ways of conveying your affection for each other. You prefer to let your behavior speak for itself and don't need to hear or say "I love you" as frequently as your partner does. She, however, says it to promote intimacy. As such she finds it reassuring when you say "I love you," and concerning when you don't.

What she really means & what she really needs

When your partner tells you she loves you, she is using relationship short-hand to intimately connect with you. She is telling you many things in this tiny statement—that she is thinking of you, she misses you, she adores you, she chooses you, and that you are the most important person in her life. What she needs in that moment is to know you feel the same way about her.

What you need to say and do

Train yourself to express your true feelings for your partner by removing any negative associations you have with hearing and saying "I love you."

- Instead of thinking, "Oh God, now she expects me to say it back," try thinking, "I am lucky to have someone who is often moved to say she loves me."
- Give your partner what she asks for—verbal reassurance—by saying "I love you, too."
- Beat her to it: Send her text messages and emails throughout the week with "I love you" or "143."

What not to say and do

It is important to take your partner's sentiment from the place it comes—genuine affection—and to not take it for granted. Consider that your partner makes herself vulnerable each time she says, "I love you." So don't become annoyed, dismissive, or make jokes at her expense.

- Avoid merely thinking, "I love you"—say it.
- Don't answer her with, "Thanks!"
- Don't accuse her of expressing love just to get something from you.
- Never make fun of her for saying "I love you."

How both of you will benefit

Saying "I love you" is like giving your partner a free and powerful gift—this little phrase can strip away defenses, crumble emotional walls and grudges, and combat insecurity by reassuring each other that you are safe and loved.

Questions to Ask Yourself

- Why do I resist saying "I love you" to my partner?
- What will it cost me to say it as often as she does?
- How will it make her feel to hear it?

Make Her
Feel Beautiful

Making your partner feel like the most
beautiful woman in the world will let you look
at other women without hurting her feelings.

The Scenario
When you notice a beautiful woman, you tend to make
comments about her body or the way she is dressed. You
also compare your partner to other women and let her
know what you like about them. This appreciation of
other women hurts your relationship, but can be fixed
without requiring you to wear blinders or ignore your
inner nature.

Situation at a Glance
- She says it is disrespectful to look at other women.
- You love your partner but can't help but admire
  other beautiful women.
- She feels threatened when you comment on other
  women's bodies.
- You are just expressing your physical preferences.

- She becomes jealous and insecure whenever other women are around.
- You want her to understand it is man's nature to notice a woman's physique.

The problem in this situation

The problem isn't that you look—it is how you look. Staring, leering, or flirting with another woman is bound to trigger your partner's insecurities. Add to that admiring comments and unflattering comparisons, and you are taking your First Amendment right to free speech a little too far! Though it may seem harmless or playful, your behavior is hurtful to your partner and threatens your relationship by encouraging jealousy, insecurity, and mistrust.

What she really means & what she really needs

According to a 2008 *PARADE* magazine poll, 60 percent of women believe their partner keeps secrets from them. This sheds some light on why your partner feels threatened by your wandering eye—she thinks you secretly want to cheat. When your partner gets upset when you admire another woman, she is really expressing that she is insecure. What she needs from you is reassurance that you find her more attractive than any other woman and that you intend to remain faithful.

What you need to say and do

If your partner is anything like the average American woman, she is approximately 5'4" and a size 14. It is likely she has struggled with her body image her entire life, given that the average model is 5'11" and weighs just 117 pounds. Help her overcome this lifetime of self-hatred by:

- Making "I have the hottest girlfriend ever!" your Facebook status for a week.
- Telling her she is the best looking woman at the party.
- Kissing her passionately in public.

What not to say and do

When you point out attractive features on other women, you plug directly into your partner's deeply ingrained insecurities. So consider your partner's feelings whenever you are tempted to compare her physical attributes with those of another woman.

- Don't treat her like a runner-up to more beautiful women. Remember, you chose her as your partner.
- Don't stare at other women in front of your partner.
- Don't suggest that your partner dress, talk, or behave like another woman.

- Avoid making even casual comparisons to other women.

How both of you will benefit
She will appreciate you making the effort to curb your impulse to gawk at beautiful women—and abstain from sharing your thoughts on their bodies—because it lets her know you respect her feelings. This does not mean you cannot admire attractive women, but rather it proves to both of you that you cherish her above all others.

Things to Realize
- Your partner will love hearing you think she is beautiful. Say it, write it, or send a text message to her every week.
- It is disrespectful to tell your partner you wish she had the physical attributes of another woman.
- Your partner depends on you to make her feel loved, respected, and physically attractive.

Explain Your Male Nature

She thinks looking at porn and going to strip clubs is disrespectful because she views sex as sacred and for people who love each other.

The Scenario

You like to read nudie magazines and go to strip clubs with the guys once in awhile, but your partner considers this a betrayal of your commitment to her. You know she is threatened by your penchant for porn, but you want her to understand what you get out of it and why it does not threaten your relationship.

Situation at a Glance

- She thinks men who view pornography are perverts.
- You enjoy perusing online pornography.
- She thinks men who go to strip clubs are cheating.
- You rarely go to strip clubs but want the option to go with the guys without having to lie about it.
- She thinks if you love her you wouldn't need porn.
- You say porn does not threaten your relationship with her.

The problem in this situation

In 2006, the porn business generated more than $13 billion, with men serving as the industry's main consumers. Because so many men partake of porn, you feel you are indulging in normal guy behavior. But your partner hates it when you go to strip clubs or look at porn because she thinks it is disrespectful. She is also afraid that you compare her body to other women's bodies; that you think of nude models when making love with her, and that eventually you will cheat. Unfortunately, you encourage her insecurities by being secretive and by not including her.

What she really means & what she really needs

Your partner views going to strip clubs as seriously disrespectful to your relationship. To her, sex is a private and special act between two people who love each other. She also believes men who go to strip clubs objectify women, most of whom are very young. She finds it disturbing that you support an industry that denigrates women and can't understand why you don't see it as wrong. What she needs is to calmly discuss her feelings about pornography without hearing you get defensive.

What you need to say and do

Engage your partner in a conversation about what you enjoy about strip clubs, magazines, and online porn. Keep it light and playful and leave out anything that may hurt her feelings. Focus on non-threatening details, like that you enjoy the male camaraderie aspect of going to strip clubs.

- Be compassionate toward your partner if she becomes upset when talking about this issue.
- Be honest about how often you want to use porn. In other words, do you want her blessing for a bachelor party or do you want to be able to visit strip clubs weekly?
- Invite your partner to go to a strip club with you— and focus your attention on her.
- Look at your favorite erotic websites together and talk about the experience.

What not to say and do

Avoid becoming defensive, defiant, or demanding when discussing pornography with your partner. The more entrenched you are in your position that it is your "right" to do these things the more it will appear to her that you have a problem—or that you are hiding something.

- Don't assert the idea that sex is just sex. Your partner cherishes sex and will see this as hurtful.
- Never lie to your partner about going to a strip club.
- Don't hide pornography or clear your browser history.
- Realize she is not trying to control you.

How both of you will benefit

Removing the mystery that surrounds your enjoyment of pornography will go a long way in calming your partner's insecurities. She will feel heard, understood, and more able to trust you, even though she may never be 100 percent comfortable with it.

Questions to Ask Yourself

- Ease your partner in with soft-core porn websites and magazines that have a story attached to sex.
- Be willing to give up your habit if your partner can't come to terms with it.
- Never hide or lie about your enjoyment of pornography.

Invest In Your Relationship

She wants you to show you are invested in the relationship by participating in the details of your mutual life.

The Scenario

You leave all the household duties, appointments, child care, pet care, and other irritating life issues for your wife to handle. You feel these are her kinds of duties, but she says it sends the message that you're not fully invested in the relationship. Participating in your mutual life demonstrates your level of commitment to your relationship to her.

Situation at a Glance

- She is offended you leave household duties to her.
- You work hard and want to relax when you get off.
- She works hard, but still finds time to run the house.
- You are more traditional and believe house-related issues are the woman's domain.
- She resents that you view housework as woman's' work.

- You don't see the point in helping, because she'll just say you did it wrong anyway.
- By the time you get around to doing a chore, she has run out of patience and done it anyway.
- You genuinely believe she is better at handling those issues.

The problem in this situation

Both partners do not feel equal ownership or responsibility toward running the household. You work, she works. Yet she also does a "second shift" at home in the evenings, and you don't. You avoid it because you believe it is her domain, think she is better at it, and expect to be criticized if you do help. To restore harmony you must share house and childcare responsibilities. On the flip side, she must learn to accept your style of participation without criticizing.

What she really means & what she really needs

The U.S. Department of Labor reports there were 68 million employed women in 2007. It is likely that most of these women are working during the day and tending to household duties at night. When your partner asks for your help, she is telling you she needs a break. She is also looking for you to demonstrate your commitment to the domestic life you've established together. She needs you to ask what you can do to help, to do it without complaint, and to make a regular contribution to tending to your mutual business.

What you need to say and do

Start out by expressing your appreciation for how your wife runs the house. Notice how well the kids are doing in school, when the house is clean, and that there is always food in your pantry. Pay attention to how your partner gets everything done, and make an effort to help where she is struggling.

- Imagine taking on all of the household duties by yourself.
- Tell her you appreciate her work by sending her a text that says, "Thanks for grocery shopping!" while she is out at the store.
- Regularly take on a task you are comfortable with, such as walking the dog, doing the laundry, or ordering dinner.
- Ask your partner to let you do it "your way."

What not to say and do

Since she has been running the show by herself, she may be resistant to your overtures to help. Don't be pushy, point out how you can do it better, or get impatient and give up.

- Don't assume because she has been doing the housework that she enjoys doing it.
- Don't exhibit a bad attitude by stomping around, slamming doors, or complaining while doing housework.
- Don't only chime in to tell her what she is doing wrong.

How both of you will benefit

A July 2006 study published in *Sex Roles: A Journal of Research*, found that women spend about half the time on housework they did in the 1960s. Men, on the other hand, have doubled their household contributions. Be one of these men. Transposing this trend into your relationship will prove you are deeply committed to your partner, and ease tensions at home.

Checklist for Action

- Ask about important appointments and attend them.
- Do at least one chore every day.
- Ask your partner how you can help, and mean it.
- Realize it is also your home, and show your investment by participating in its everyday operations.

Tips & Exercises

Use the following activities, tips and advice to enhance your commitment and fidelity.

Try This at Home

More than 2,300 surveys about what makes a successful marriage have been conducted since January 2003. Interestingly, honesty and trust are 2 out of the top 3 most important components of a marriage consistently reported across all surveys. It is clear that honesty and trust are key to any lasting relationship, so you'll want to make sure you and your partner have plenty of both.

To show your partner you are honest and trustworthy, try making the following regular components of your personality:

- Call when you say you're going to call.
- Come home at the time you specified—or call to let her know you'll be late.

- Don't lie, ever.
- Admit the hardest truths. Examples include:
  - You want to travel without her.
  - You are angry with her that she quit her job, lied to you, drank too much at a party, embarrassed you, or some other grievance.
  - Another woman hit on you.
  - You lost a large sum of money in the stock market, gambling, or a personal investment.
- Don't stay out all night.
- Be where you said you were going to be.
- Don't keep your friendship with another woman a secret.
- Invite her to happy hours with your coworkers now and then.
- Follow through on favors she asks for that you agree to, such as throwing out pornography, losing the number of an old girlfriend, or quitting smoking.

Openness & Communication

Women who talk a lot may be on to something. According to a study conducted by psychologists at the University of Michigan and the University of California, San Diego, just 10 minutes of talking per day improves memory and test performance.

Lead author Oscar Ybarra said the study, which was published in the February 2008 issue of *Personality and Social Psychology Bulletin*, revealed that "the higher the level of participants' social interaction, the better their cognitive functioning." Other researchers point to talking as a way to reduce stress and improve heart health. One could say, then, that for women, talk is matter of survival.

Women talk to share their joy in times of happiness and excitement and to unload their woes when times are bad. Both excuses to yap yield the same result; talking about the good and the bad makes them feel better. Talk for women functions both as a therapeutic antidote to negative emotions as well as a way to amplify their happiness when life is good.

Being the natural talkers that they are, women often complain they are with men who do not talk enough. These women feel the burden to carry a conversation is on them, and are unsatisfied by short one- or two-word answers to questions or topics of discussion. They internalize this silence as symbolizing a problem with the relationship and wonder who their man would really rather be talking to.

Many women also complain they have to repeat themselves because their male partners don't listen to them when they say, ask, or comment the first time. Many of them feel as 1947 Nobel Prize winner Andre Gide put it when he said, "Everything has been said before, but since nobody listens we have to keep going back and beginning all over again." That your partner repeats herself is probably a chief complaint you have about her, yet she is doing it because she is not getting the message, through either your words or your actions, that you heard her the first time.

Figure out why she does what she does:

1. She talks to make an intimate connection with you.

2. She repeatedly tells the same story, not because she is looking for you to solve a problem, but because she is working it "out loud" on her own.

3. She talks to you because you are a witness to her life.

Improving your listening and communication skills, therefore, is good for both of you. If she feels heard the first time she will be less likely to repeat herself. If she feels engaged in quality conversation, she will feel less compelled to nag you to talk to her.

Make An
Effort to Talk

When you are silent for too long she thinks
something is wrong, even when it's not.

The Scenario
Your partner complains that she feels like she has no
idea who you are anymore, because you never talk about
your feelings. She interprets your silence as evidence
that you are not interested in talking to her. You feel
like nothing has changed and have no idea where this
is coming from. It's true there are times when you don't
have much to say, but it's simply because you don't have
much to say.

Situation at a Glance
- She is concerned you are growing apart.
- You are not in the habit of talking about your
  feelings.
- She wants you to "let her in."
- You don't know what that means.

- She thinks your silence as a sign the relationship is failing.
- You are annoyed because everything was fine, but now you are suddenly in a fight about nothing.

The problem in this situation

You and your partner have different ideas about what conversation is for. She, like most women, uses it to enhance her interpersonal connections and to maintain relationships. You, like most men, talk to assert your status or to make convincing arguments. Gender communications expert Deborah Tannen refers to these differences as "rapport talk" versus "report talk."

What she really means & what she really needs

Telling you that she feels as if she doesn't know you anymore indicates that she senses a distance. Getting you to talk about your feelings is her way of closing this gap. She needs reassurance that nothing is wrong, that you still love her, and that your silence does not indicate you are angry, bored, or having an affair.

What you need to say and do

At times you may agree with writer Oscar Wilde, who said, "Women are meant to be loved, not understood." But for the sake of your relationship, you'll have to do both. Try to understand where she is coming from and give her your attention.

- Schedule time to talk so you do not feel ambushed and put on the defensive.
- Consider whether your partner has picked up on a particular vibe you've put out lately.
- Express anger or frustration so it doesn't build.
- Reconnect with your partner on her terms by agreeing to one "deep" conversation per month.
- Say to her, "I want to understand your point of view, but I am having a hard time."

What not to say and do

As far as you are concerned, relationships can pretty much run on autopilot once a commitment is made. Aside from special occasions, like birthdays and anniversaries, you see no reason to reiterate the obvious: you love each other and want to be together. Avoid sharing that last part with your partner—it is not romantic, and also indicates that you've become complacent.

- Don't say she is acting crazy, irrational, silly, or like a nag.
- Don't say you have nothing to say to her.
- Don't blow her off when she wants to talk.

- Avoid becoming upset, angry, dismissive, and/or defensive.

How both of you will benefit

Talking to each other is good for your health, according to a study led by Dr. Andrea Horn of the University of Fribourg, Switzerland. Sharing information with your partner promotes feelings of intimacy and improves the quality of the relationship. The study revealed that talking to your partner—even about the mundane details of your work day—helps to regulate emotions and relieves stress. However, only the person who does the talking reaps these benefits. In order for both partners to benefit, both must participate in the conversation.

Questions to Ask Yourself

- Is it such a big deal to chat every day with my partner?
- What is my body language when my partner talks to me?
- What will I gain by sharing my feelings? What will I lose by shrugging off her efforts to connect through conversation?

Take Time
to Make Up

She needs to see an argument through
to its resolution and then make up
to feel like things are OK.

The Scenario

In the midst of an argument, you throw your hands up and shout, "That's the end of it! I'm done talking about this." You just want to move on and forget all about the fight, but your partner feels like you shut her down without working through the problem. Taking time to make up from the fight makes it easier to put whatever you were fighting about behind you both for good.

Situation at a Glance

- She is upset because you ended the discussion.
- You are frustrated and want the conversation to just end.
- She has much more to stay and will not let it drop.
- You do not want the argument to escalate, because you are afraid you will say something you will regret.

- She won't go to bed until everything is resolved.
- You want to sleep on it, forget about it, and start fresh tomorrow.

The problem in this situation

It starts out as a discussion, turns into an argument, and escalates into a power struggle. You and your partner both try to wrest control of an argument using very different techniques. Your way of controlling the situation is to shut it down, while her method is to talk in circles until an agreement is reached. University of Utah professor of psychology Tim Smith believes men and women may be physically predisposed to react this way. Smith learned from his research that the heart health of a man suffers when he feels as though he is losing control—such as when he is involved in an argument he thinks he cannot win. However, Smith also learned that a woman's heart health is negatively affected by unresolved issues—since she views herself as the "manager" of the relationship.

What she really means & what she really needs

As the self-appointed manager of your relationship, your partner is evaluating your "job performance." And like any manager, whenever she notices room for improvement she will bring it to your attention. She frequently "checks in" to reassure herself that the relationship is operating at its optimum level—because when it's not, she feels like a failure.

What you need to say and do

For starters, promote yourself to co-manager of the relationship. Participate in or even start discussions about the relationship so you are not always on the receiving end of your partner's feedback. Next, be assertive and calm instead of passive-aggressive during arguments. Stick around until the end of the argument. She will notice all of your efforts and appreciate that you control your frustration.

- Take deep breaths to stay calm and rational.
- Think before you speak.
- Set a timer during an argument, and end the conversation when the alarm goes off.

What not to say and do

Your partner wants to come to an agreement, to build consensus, and to feel like you are on the same team. You just want to get as far from the situation as possible, but this is counterproductive. Imagine the argument is a football, you are the quarterback and your partner is the wide receiver. When you storm off it's like you take the football with you, leaving her alone on the playing field with no hope of getting a touchdown for the team.

- Don't become so angry that you can't talk rationally.
- Don't assume that just because you walk away from the argument that it is over.
- Don't assert your point of view so there isn't room for hers.

How both of you will benefit

Learning how to argue with your partner is perhaps the most important relationship skill you can develop. Setting time limits, having willingness to compromise, and letting the small stuff fall by the wayside allows for healthy expression of disappointment, anger, and disagreement.

Things to Realize

- Arguments are just blips on your relationship's radar.
- The point of arguing is to ultimately negotiate the best possible outcome with your partner.

Be Forthright

Your spouse finds meaning in the details—and suspicion in their omission.

The Scenario
You neglect to mention that a female coworker is traveling with you on a work assignment to another city. Your partner finds out and assumes you are hiding something. You try to explain that you didn't mention it because you didn't think it was important, but your partner thinks something is up. Making these kinds of details known well in advance will help you both avoid tension and mistrust.

Situation at a Glance
- She places value on information you did not provide.
- You left out lots of mundane details about the trip, and don't see why she is stuck on this one.
- She is suspicious of your motives.
- You think she is overreacting.

- She wants an explanation for why you didn't tell her.
- You don't have one, because there isn't one.

The problem in this situation

It may seem as though your partner agrees with American humorist Helen Rowland, who once said, "Telling lies is a fault in a boy, an art in a lover, an accomplishment in a bachelor, and second-nature in a married man." Like most women, she believes that the truth of a story resides in the details—or in this case, in their omission. You, like most men, don't care about detail, so you often neglect to relay them. Even so, you consider yourself to be truthful. This difference of opinion about "truth" can be toxic in relationships that suffer from a lack of trust.

What she really means & what she really needs

When your partner accuses you of lying (translation: leaving out important details) she is saying she thinks you have something to hide. Her mistrust is based on her interest in the details. She also feels threatened by the mystery surrounding your female coworker. She needs to be reassured of your honesty, loyalty, and fidelity by having you fill in the blanks.

What you need to say and do

You can only do so much to convince your partner that

you are telling the truth when you leave out (what she views as) key parts of the story. Hopefully, reminding your spouse of your record of honesty, commitment, and faithfulness will be enough to convince her you have nothing to hide. Remind her that since you prefer to receive information in concise tidbits, you also deliver it that way.

- Make eye contact with your partner. It lets her know you have nothing to hide.
- Remind her of other times you left out innocuous details to show this is not unusual, but rather how you tell stories.
- Speak slowly and calmly, and make sure your body language matches your tone.

What not to say and do
The worst thing you can do is to become defensive or angry—these are signals that you are in fact hiding something. Though your partner's lack of trust in you is frustrating, stay calm during the discussion. Otherwise, she will go from suspecting you have something to hide to being convinced of it.

- Never say anything like the following: "If you think I'm cheating on you, I might as well and get the benefits along with the punishment!"

- Don't let the discussion to stray from the issue, which is that you don't share details you think are unimportant.
- Never tell your spouse you omit details because you "knew" she would get mad, or because they are none of her business.

How both of you will benefit

A healthy compromise will be reached when you agree to provide more information and your partner learns to expect fewer details. Changing the rules for how you share information with each other in this way will minimize the hostility fueled by miscommunication. It also allows for healthy conflict resolution—the most important component of all loving relationships, according to Dr. James Dobson, author of *The Complete Marriage & Family Home Reference Guide*.

Things to Realize

- How you communicate information to your partner is the issue, not that you have a co-ed business trip.

Learn to Just Listen

When your partner talks about a problem with you, she is not always looking for a solution.

The Scenario

Your girlfriend had a huge fight with her best friend. She is depressed for days before she finally decides to talk to you about what happened. You advise her to cut ties with her friend and move on. Her response is to get angry with you and complain that you never "just listen." You have heard her complain about this friend before, and don't understand why she doesn't want to do anything about the problem already.

Situation at a Glance

- She is deeply upset over a fight with her friend.
- You don't understand why she lets things like this affect her so deeply.
- She needs to talk about what happened to feel better.

- You want to fix the problem.
- She is annoyed by your advice.
- You don't understand why she is mad at you now.

The problem in this situation
The reason your partner quickly switched from forlorn to fierce is that she wants you to listen and console—not to offer advice or talk badly about her friend. If she doesn't ask for your opinion, it is safe to assume she doesn't want it. More than advice, she wants an outlet for her sadness and frustration.

What she really means & what she really needs
When your partner confides in you about her troubles with a friend, she needs you to listen and sympathize. Though there are many times in your relationship where she will resent you for talking too little, this won't be one of them. As French playwright Marcel Achard once put it, "Women like silent men. They think they're listening." Keep the conversation moving with questions about how she's feeling rather than with advice about what she should do.

What you need to say and do
Validate her feelings and remain neutral. Understand that when she calls her friend a nasty name it is not an

invitation for you to join in by slamming her best pal. In fact, women remain loyal to their friendships even when they're fighting. The best way for you to help her through this problem is to be a good listener.

- Use active listening to show her you're paying attention. Repeat back what you think she's saying. For example, "It sounds like Beth really hurt your feelings."
- Instead of giving advice, ask her questions. "How did that make you feel?" "What happened next?" or "Why do you think she said that?" are all good ones to start with.
- Squeeze her hand or put your arm around her while you listen.
- Let her talk until she is done.

What not to say and do

When your partner talks about a problem, you must quash your desire to be helpful—unless you want to become her next target! According to a 2008 study conducted by the Relationship Services Organization in New Zealand, more than 40 percent of women polled blamed the number of disagreements they had with their partner on their man's inability to listen.

- Avoid giving solutions or advice unless your partner directly asks, "What do you think I should do?"
- Don't downplay her problem or say she is overreacting.
- Don't insult her friend. They will make up and then your girlfriend will resent your comments.

How both of you will benefit

Men who understand their partner's need to vent have it made. They no longer have to work to find sense and logic in the details of their partner's problem in order to come up with a fitting solution. They are also more patient when their partner repeats the same story over and over. These men finally get it—the solution is to simply let her talk, and then she will feel better. Removing your resistance to this method of expression benefits you both; your partner gets to work through her issue and you avoid becoming her next target.

Things to Realize
- Talking is therapeutic for your partner.
- If she wants your advice she will ask for it.
- Questions, rather than advice, will be appreciated.

Tips &
Exercises

Use the following activities,
tips and advice to enhance your
openness and communication.

Get to Know Each Other ... Again

After years together, it can be hard to imagine there is
anything you don't know about your partner. But the
business of life often gets in the way of keeping current
with each other's shifting opinions, goals, values, and
desires. In fact, people in a relationship undergo many
changes over time. But since these can be hard to see on
a day-to-day basis, they are often overlooked entirely by
partners. Think of your partner like a tree. You can't see
her day-to-day growth, but over the course of 1, 5, or 10
years, her many changes are quite obvious.

Use this exercise to enrich your relationship. It will help
you reconnect with the person your partner has become.

Answer these questions, and then ask your partner to do the same. Use your answers as a jumping off point to get a conversation started.

Ask her ...
1. What are your top 3 priorities in life, in order of importance?
2. What worries you?
3. What makes you happy?
4. What sexual fantasies do you have that I can help you fulfill?
5. Are you satisfied with your job?
6. Do you ever think about having a/another child?
7. What matters most when it comes to our children's education?
8. Do you harbor any resentment toward me for anything I've done?
9. Where do you see yourself in 5, 10, and 25 years? What about us as a couple? What about us as a family?
10. What is most important to you: financial security, personal happiness, or good health? Why?

Priorities
& Values

Aside from infidelity, there may be no bigger threat to a relationship than a divergent value system.

When a couple finally realizes that their core beliefs no longer match, one of two things can happen: they retreat to their separate corners, grow apart, and eventually divorce; or they do as Charles and Emma Darwin did—and agree to disagree.

Charles Darwin and Emma Wedgwood were married in 1839. They remained together until his death in 1882, despite dramatic differences of opinion on God and religion. Emma, a devout Christian, struggled with Darwin's research. She was deeply offended by his book, *On the Origin of the Species*, in which he outlined his theory of evolution.

Their relationship suffered further stress when their 10 year-old daughter Annie died unexpectedly, causing Darwin to declare he was an agnostic.

Though Charles and Emma wrestled with their different belief systems throughout their marriage, letters between the two revealed that it was how they handled these problems that saved their marriage. For example, in one letter Emma gently urged Charles to avoid applying scientific thought to ideas that "are likely to be above our comprehension." In turn, rather than becoming angry or calling her a fool for her beliefs, he wrote, "When I am dead, know that many times, I have kissed and cried over this. C. D."

It is very common for couples to diverge on at least some matters of morality, value, and priority. It is likely these differences have sparked many an argument.

Figure out why she does what she does:

1. She values family above all else and wants you to do the same.

2. Her priorities directly support the family unit, and she expects the same from you.

3. She will tolerate different philosophies in the home as long as you respect hers.

When conflicts over values and priorities arise in your marriage, recall how Charles and Emma Darwin treated their fundamental differences with compassion and respect. Consider why it is your partner holds the beliefs she does; look at them from her perspective with fresh eyes, and find at least one valid reason for holding such a viewpoint.

Finally, remember to hear each other out as Charles and Emma did, without ridicule or judgment. Allow your foundation of friendship, love, and mutual attraction to remain strong, regardless of your differences of opinion.

Honor
Her Faith

Know that religion becomes increasingly important to women after they have children.

The Scenario
After your first child was born your wife announced that she wanted to have him baptized. You were surprised by this, because your partner never went to church or discussed her faith before. Now she wants the kids to go to Sunday School, and you are not sure. You are reluctant to join a church, because you are not religious and do not want to make the time commitment.

Situation at a Glance
- She wants your children to be brought up knowing religion.
- You have always viewed organized religion as a farce.
- She says exposure to religion will help build character and a sense of family.

- You think your family already has these qualities.
- She does not understand your opposition.
- You don't want to teach your kids ideas you yourself are not comfortable with or don't fully believe.

The problem in this situation
You and your wife were always in sync with the big issues in life. You agreed that religion was not a top priority for either of you—until now. Your partner seems to have changed her mind about religion's role in her life, and she worked it all out on her own without discussing it with you. The closeness you developed during the early years as a family is suddenly threatened by her strong desire to bring religion into the picture, regardless of how you feel about it.

What she really means & what she really needs
One reason women "discover" religion after childbirth is that their self-esteem becomes inexorably tied to their motherhood job performance. Feeling part of a larger, organized community offers both an affirming support network and a built-in value system. As *Christian Women Today* contributor Karen L. Schenk notes, moms that have an anchor outside of their children—such as a relationship with God—are less prone to the ups and downs of new motherhood.

What you need to say and do

Any time a couple experiences a split in shared values it can feel like you are moving in different directions. Try not to think this way. Instead, view your partner's attraction to religion as a motherhood-inspired desire to develop her spirituality for the benefit of her child.

- Ask her to explain why religion is important to her, and take her answer seriously.
- Support her reasons for wanting to join a congregation—community, values, structure, and free childcare.
- Evaluate your reasons for opposing religion and calmly discuss them with your partner.
- Compromise. For example, agree to attend church on holidays, but ask that she hold off on a religious education until the kids are old enough to decide for themselves.

What not to say and do

Your partner's value system has changed, and to preserve the marriage you will have to find a way to deal with it. When one partner is called to follow God and the other is not, the relationship can still thrive as long as they respect each other. However, as Susan Vogt of AmericanCatholic.org warns, when couples mock each others' values "tension will be a constant companion." With that in mind:

- Never mock your wife's urge to explore her spirituality.
- Don't oppose religion just to exert your authority.
- Don't be afraid to explore religion's pros and cons as a family.

How both of you will benefit

Your relationship will be stronger for the attempts you make to communicate your core beliefs. Even though hers may differ from before she had a baby, she is still the same person. Her newfound interest in affiliating the family with a religion is just an extension of her desire to make connections. Treating this issue seriously and with respect will deepen your bond and bring you closer together.

Questions to Ask Your Partner

- When did you change your mind about religion?
- How can we compromise on the subject of religion?

Put Your Family First

Your partner expects you to put her and the family before any other commitments.

The Scenario

You are invited to watch a football game at your buddy's house. Unfortunately, it falls on the same day as an outing your partner planned for the family weeks ago. You'd rather go to the game and have trouble understanding why it's a big deal to reschedule the family outing. She accuses you of caring more about football than your family.

Situation at a Glance

- She planned a special day for the family weeks ago.
- You forgot and accepted an invite to watch a game.
- She's mad you forgot about the plans and hurt that you would rather watch the game.
- You think you can do this family activity any time, but the game is only on this one day.

- She says that your priorities are in the wrong place.
- You think she is overreacting.

The problem in this situation

Your partner feels pretty low on your list of priorities. Not only did you forget she planned a special day for the family, but you also made it clear that you would prefer watching the game to spending time with her and the kids. It's not that you don't love your family, but your wife demands you spend all your free time doing dad stuff, and you need a break now and then.

What she really means & what she really needs

Your partner is hurt by the ease with which you are willing to blow off this family event. She believes, as Mahatma Gandhi did that "action expresses priorities." She planned the outing, carved out time from her schedule, and let you know about it in advance. The energy she put into this activity is just one of many ways she shows the family is her top priority. Your wife needs to be reminded that family is at the top of your list.

What you need to say and do

Try explaining the way you feel in a way that is less offensive than, "I'd rather go to the game, what's the big deal?" Apologize for forgetting family day and for misrepresenting your priorities—assure her your family is most important to you. Offer to skip the game, but only if you won't resent missing it. Indeed, if you harbor resentment over the issue, you inadvertently confirm your partner's worst fear—that you are in fact not interested in making the family your top priority.

- If you can't stand to miss the game ask your partner for a rain check and write the new date in your calendar immediately.
- Appreciate your family—you have a family that loves you and wants to spend time together. This is a good thing!
- Surprise your partner by taking it on yourself to plan the next fun-filled family activity.

What not to say and do
Avoid saying anything that will make your partner feel worse, such as "Family outings are boring, the game is more fun," "You just want to control me," or, "None of the other guys have to spend time with their families." Your goal is to de-escalate the situation by restoring the family's status as your top priority.

- Don't tell your friends your wife "made" you spend time with the family. Going on the family outing with this mentality defeats the whole purpose.

- Don't dread doing things with your family! Feel lucky that you get to be with your wife and kids.
- Don't forget to keep an accurate calendar so this doesn't happen again.

How both of you will benefit

Sometimes it takes an argument, separation, or tragedy for people to reset their priorities and focus on their family. Thankfully, this was just a small incident that led to a medium-sized argument that brought you back to your biggest priority—your family.

Checklist for Action

Three ways I can show my family I appreciate them are:

1._____

2._____

3._____

Spend Quality Time Together

She judges the amount of time you spend with her and the kids as proof of where your priorities lie.

The Scenario

On weekends you like to work on home improvement projects or go out with friends to play sports or grab a few beers. You always make time to eat breakfast and dinner with your kids, but your partner still complains you don't spend enough time together— both as a family and as a couple.

Situation at a Glance

- She wants you to want to spend more time together.
- You work hard all week and value your free time on weekends.
- She values her free time too, but also time spent with you.
- She accuses you of rushing through meals to get to "the next thing."

- You don't understand what she is talking about.
- She feels rejected when you don't make "quality" time for her.

The problem in this situation

You and your partner have vastly different ideas about what constitutes spending time together. The root of this problem is that men and women view reality from different perspectives. Men quantify the actual amount of time spent together, whereas women measure the quality of time spent in each other's company.

What she really means & what she really needs

William Faulkner once wrote, "Clocks slay time...time is dead as long as it is being clicked off by little wheels; only when the clock stops does time come to life." Faulkner's words likely apply to how your wife views your time at home. When you're together, your wife wants you to engage in meaningful companionship, not punch the clock and do a "shift." Rushing through breakfast to get to the next thing makes your wife feel as though time spent with family is not a top priority for you.

What you need to say and do

Men that pop in and out of their home lives send the following message: "My life is full of equally important activities, and you are but one of many of them!" On the surface, this may not seem like a bad thing, but it is bad for your relationship over time. It is based on assumptions, such as your partner will be there whenever you want her to be; her time is less valuable than yours; and your children are your wife's primary responsibility. You become a visitor, a surprise guest in your own family, and much less involved in your household responsibilities than you should be.

- Think of quality time spent with your family as an investment in everyone's long-term happiness.
- Take the initiative and suggest a weekly activity the whole family will enjoy—including you.
- Dedicate one full weekend day to spending with your family and ask that the other weekend day be open to doing other things if the opportunity arises.

What not to say and do

In *Stupid Things Men Say and Women Do*, author Kathleen Meyers says that women are famous for jumping to conclusions. When the relationship doesn't quite measure up, your partner will create her own version of why unless you stop her by using good sense in your words and actions.

With this in mind:

- Don't do or say anything to confirm your wife's belief that your priorities are out of whack.
- Avoid warping her perception with mistakes, such as forgetting family commitments.
- Don't forget to make time for you and your wife alone.

How both of you will benefit
There is no downside to making a bigger effort to spending more time with your family. Everyone wins when husband, wife, and children make it a priority to become a close-knit group of people who enjoy spending time together.

Questions to Ask Yourself
- What does the time you spend together tell your kids about your relationship with your wife?
- Would you be satisfied if your child's spouse spent as little/as much time with her as you do?

Balance Work and Home

Women often feel neglected and taken for granted when men work long hours and are away from home.

The Scenario
You constantly take on new projects at work and, as a result, work long hours and are frequently away on business. Your partner accuses you of avoiding her by burying yourself in your work. You wish she could understand how important your career is to you and see that you are working hard to benefit both of you.

Situation at a Glance
- She feels sidelined by your career.
- You worked hard to get where you are at your job and must continue to do so to stay there.
- She says she would rather have less money and more time with you.
- You believe she thinks she means that but point out she has gotten used to the lifestyle your hard work provides.

- She's lonely and wants you to scale back your hours.
- You think she doesn't value hard work as much as you do.
- She accuses you of hiding from her at work.
- You love your wife but are driven by a need to conquer, succeed, and provide.

The problem in this situation

You have the same problem as the men and women who participated in a 2003 Pew Research Center global survey on gender gaps. Survey results showed that worldwide, women focus most of their energy on issues that affect their families, and men are more concerned with their careers.

What she really means & what she really needs

You believe that the measure of a man is his work, and your philosophy can be summed up by the following Aristotle quote: "We are what we repeatedly do. Excellence, then, is not an act, but a habit." Your partner, however, is more of a romantic and identifies with what Emily Dickinson said in one of her poems: "That Love is all there is, is all we know of Love; it is enough." Your wife needs to know that you value her love as much—if not more—than your work. You can do this by making her a priority that is at least equal to your career.

What you need to say and do

Arguing the value of work versus marriage draws a line in the sand of your relationship. One side is for work and the other is love. You and your partner are standing on either side of the line. But the idea that one must choose between work or love is false. So take the first step toward erasing this line by allowing work and love to blend together. Do this by creating a shared life with similar priorities.

- Commit to working 40 hours a week unless there is a special project that needs extra time.
- Create a "no-work" zone in your home. Make this either a physical space or a time which no work will be done.
- Make a weekly lunch date with your partner.

What not to say and do

Your goal for resolving this issue is to live a more balanced life. With that in mind, don't gravitate too far toward either your work or home life and don't get mean to prove a point. In other words, do not do any of the following:

- Don't threaten to quit your job.
- Don't take more work to avoid seeing your spouse.

- Don't turn cruel or manipulative by citing her faults as the reason you stay away from the home.
- Don't denigrate her line of work—especially if she is a stay-at-home mom—to elevate the value of yours.

How both of you will benefit

When approached with tact, respect, and compassion, hashing out your priorities is the perfect way to realign your relationship. It reminds you of all you have in common and challenges you both to see the other's perspective. All of this hard work pays off in a more loving, mature relationship. As Antoine Saint-Exupery once wrote, "Love does not consist in gazing at each other, but in looking outward together in the same direction."

Checklist for Action

- Be home for dinner at least 3 or 4 nights a week.
- Be selective when taking on new projects at work.
- Use words and actions to show your family is a priority.

Tips & Exercises

Use the following activities, tips and advice to enhance your priorities and values.

Thirty Compliments to Show She is Your Top Priority

A woman craves affirmation from her man that he is moved by her in some way. Email, text, or simply pay verbal compliments often and be genuine in their delivery. Tell her ...

1. I love your smile.
2. Your laugh is contagious!
3. Your eyes are beautiful.
4. You look gorgeous!
5. You are so funny.
6. Your body is incredible.
7. You are really great at your job.
8. You always have such good ideas.
9. You are the best cook ever!

10. You amaze me.
11. You're a great mom.
12. You are the best wife/girlfriend ever!
13. You have the cutest butt.
14. I love watching your hands while you work.
15. I appreciate your feedback.
16. I would be lost without you.
17. You really know how to put an outfit together.
18. Marrying you was the best thing I've ever done.
19. You really light up a room.
20. Your scent drives me wild!
21. I can't stop thinking about your body.
22. Your hair smells wonderful.
23. I love your new haircut!
24. You are a great friend.
25. You are home to me.
26. I could kiss you for hours.
27. You have the softest skin.
28. Your neck is so elegant.
29. I love coming home to you.
30. You're the smartest woman I've ever known.

Money &
Finances

A 2008 study called "What Women Want: A National Survey of Priorities and Concerns," conducted for the YWCA USA by Princeton Survey Research Associate International (PSRAI), found that the overwhelming majority of women cited "personal economic problems" as the biggest threat they face over the next 10 years.

Seventy percent of women worried about their lack of retirement savings, while 68 percent feared major illness and medical expenses. Ninety-two percent of women also said that President Obama and Congress should make the economic crisis the top priority in their first year in Washington. American women, it seems, are feeling the economic pinch as acutely as their male companions.

The near collapse of the housing market and credit and banking industries in 2007 to 2009 upped the ante for dealing with financial stressors in homes across the globe. More households found themselves with reduced income, loss of savings, or with one person out of work entirely. In fact, the U.S. Department of

Labor reported the unemployment rate had jumped to 9 percent in early 2009 as layoffs continued and factories and businesses downsized or shut down completely. As economists and government officials try to figure out why the bubble burst and how to save the economy, families must learn new ways to cope with their personal financial losses—and figure out how to rebuild their version of the American Dream.

With so much at stake, it is more important than ever for couples learn how to talk about money. This stressful and sensitive topic is challenging for almost all couples, and especially women.

Figure out why she does what she does:

1. Spending money makes her feel in control, normalizes her economic circumstances, and serves as emotional "retail therapy."

2. Saving money and investing conservatively make her feel safe.

3. She views gift-giving as an opportunity to demonstrate intimate knowledge and affection—not wealth.

Tread carefully when discussing money matters with your partner. Though it is the number one stressor American couples face, they must face it together. Learning to fight fair when stress is at its peak can help. Dr. James Dobson, author of *The Complete Marriage & Family Home Reference Guide*, notes that couples who fight fair are equipped to deal with difficult issues, argue on-topic, and do not expect to see eye-to-eye on every problem. When all else fails, remember what Benjamin Franklin once said about money: "Money never made a man happy yet, nor will it. The more a man has, the more he wants. Instead of filling a vacuum, it makes one."

She Needs
Retail Therapy

Women use shopping to improve their moods and to exert control over their finances.

The Scenario
Your partner comes home with a new pair of shoes at least once a month—even though she already has a closet full of shoes in great condition! You figured out that she spends more than $1,000 on shoes annually. You say it's a waste of money—she says it's important to her self-esteem.

Situation at a Glance
- She feels good about herself when she shops for shoes.
- You think shopping is a frivolous activity unless you truly need something.
- She always "needs" a new pair of shoes for some event.
- You don't understand why she can't just wear a pair she already owns and stop spending money.

ou are trying to control her when you
op spending.

nk she's addicted to accumulating new things.

The problem in this situation

The Wharton School's Jay H. Baker Retail Initiative and the Verde Group put it best with the title of their 2007 study, "Men Buy, Women Shop." The study revealed that men go on a mission to buy a specific product, while women shop to have an emotional experience. These reasons are so different, it's no wonder you and your wife don't see eye-to-eye on shopping.

What she really means & what she really needs

The women's consumer advocacy organization Women-Certified reports that women spend $4 trillion per year on various products and services. This means women are responsible for a whopping 83 percent of overall U.S. consumer spending. In other words, your wife is perfectly normal! She shops because she likes it. It makes her feel good, and she feels validated by the experience of spending her own money. Still, it's important that she understand her shopping budget must match the financial reality in your household.

What you need to say and do

Try to understand your wife's psychology when she shops. She tries on shoes that make her feel attractive; sales associates pay her compliments ("Your husband will go wild when he sees you in those shoes!"); and she gets to purchase new things, which establishes her financial independence from you. Even if you are actually footing the bill, in the moment, the ritual of paying for her purchases makes her feel empowered. Treat her like an adult by working together on a reasonable shopping budget.

- Understand that women buy new clothes to please their partners and keep them interested.
- Compliment her on how she looks in her new shoes before discussing the financial impact of the purchase.
- Work together to come up with a realistic budget that includes a shoe-shopping stipend.

What not to say and do

Since your partner probably does most of the family's shopping, don't try to wrestle for control in this one area. Indeed, *Business Week* magazine reports in, "I Am Woman, Hear Me Shop," that women make 80 percent of all buying decisions for the home.

- Avoid making demands about how your partner spends money. Instead, make suggestions.

- Don't judge the value of her purchases by your standards.
- Don't treat her like a child by threatening to take away credit cards or by putting her on an allowance, especially if she contributes equally to the household income.

How both of you will benefit

Calmly discussing the financial impact of your partner's shopping demonstrates maturity and respect. This issue also serves as a welcome reminder that your marriage is an adult partnership founded on equality, free will, and compromise.

Checklist for Action

- Before discussing financial matters, be calm, organized, and in control of your emotions.
- Be open to understanding her rationale.
- Understand that your partner is a capable, reasonable adult, and treat her that way when you bring up financial concerns.

Invest in Shared Experiences

She views going out to dinner as paying for more than just food and drink. She thinks of it as paying for a complete experience.

The Scenario

Your wife or girlfriend likes to go out for fine dining or have cocktails at a swanky new bar once a week. You see it as indulging in an unnecessary expense on stuff that is fleeting. Some cocktails cost as much as your whole lunch did! Even though you both wanted to have a nice evening together, you inevitably end up in an argument over where to go and how much to pay for your food and drink.

Situation at a Glance

- She likes to go to a nice dinner out "just because."
- You think spending money on drinks and dinner once a week costs too much.
- She looks forward to going out with you all week.
- You dread it because you know she is going to pick an expensive restaurant.

- She considers spending money on cocktails and fine food as a great experience, an investment in your relationship.
- You think it's a waste of money, because you don't own anything new when it's over.

The problem in this situation

The Employment Policy Foundation reports that the number of women earning $100,000 or more tripled between 1995 and 2005. As a result women are shifting their buying power into the luxury market, which includes fine dining. It is likely that your partner can now afford to pay for dining experiences that were once reserved for the wealthy, and it makes her feel great to do so. You, on the other hand, believe money should be saved, invested, or spent on tangible items and vacations—not thrown away on overpriced meals.

What she really means & what she really needs

Marriage therapist Barton Goldsmith writes in "Income and Compatibility" that "couples find it harder to talk about money than sex." Discussing money ruins the experience for your wife, just as talking about sex can ruin the mood. Your partner wants you to accept that you are paying for an overall experience—good service, great food, top-shelf drinks, atmosphere, and the general good time and conversation you will share.

What you need to say and do

Financial disagreements are serious business in a relationship. David Bach, author of *Smart Couples Finish First*, notes that finances consistently end up as one of the top four reasons cited for getting a divorce. Keep this in mind and maintain control over your temper whenever you bring up financial discussions with your partner.

- Remember that you are on the same side.
- Budget an amount to go out to fancy restaurants once or twice a month and to moderately priced places in between.
- Agree to let her spend a similar amount on dining as you do on sports equipment, music, or other regular purchases.

What not to say and do

You may never agree with your partner that regularly splurging on dining is worth the money. But you can agree to disagree without turning into a bully. When men are unable to change their partner's mind, some resort to school-yard bully tactics, such as name-calling, threats, and intimidation.

- Don't call your partner nasty or sarcastic names.
- Don't threaten to separate your bank accounts.

- Don't try to assert your authority over your partner.
- Don't be taken advantage of. You should not be working 2 jobs just to support her luxurious tastes.

How both of you will benefit

Fights about money can destroy a relationship. But when a couple agrees to stick to a budget, to spend in the open, to be held accountable for mistakes, and to allow each other financial independence, you have a true partnership. Setting financial boundaries together—and sticking to them—encourages financial responsibility and helps to stabilize your relationship.

Questions to Ask Your Partner

- Will you agree to limit expensive restaurant outings to once or twice a month?
- Will you agree on a "fancy night out" budget?
- Do you understand why it's hard for me to spend $100 or more on food and drink for two people for one night?

Give the Right Gift

Women don't care how much a gift costs. Show you've been paying attention by giving her a present that reflects her personality.

The Scenario

You bought your wife an expensive new car stereo for her birthday. When she opened her gift, she was clearly disappointed. You are confused, because you recently had a conversation with her about how the car's sound system needed an upgrade. Plus, it is a high-quality system that anyone should be thrilled to own.

Situation at a Glance

- She was visibly disappointed in her gift after opening it.
- You were shocked, because you spent a lot of money on it.
- She accused you of buying yourself a present and passing it off as something for her.
- You are mad she would accuse you of something so selfish.

- She wants you to return it.
- You think you might as well keep it now and put it in your car.

The problem in this situation

Consumer psychologist Margaret Rucker confirms that having different expectations for gift giving and receiving tends to fall along gender lines. You, like most men, believe a gift should be economical, of good quality, and practical. For you, the car stereo fit this bill. You assumed that because the old one needed to be replaced, your partner would be happy to receive a new one. On the other hand, your wife values the emotional connection and intimacy that is exhibited by giving and receiving presents. She wanted to be swept off her feet by your thoughtfulness. Instead, she was hit over the head by your practicality.

What she really means & what she really needs

Like most women, your wife over-thinks everything, from what to eat for breakfast to why you didn't say "I love you" before hanging up the phone. Dr. Susan Nolen-Hoeksema, a professor of psychology at the University of Michigan calls such women "ruminators." They analyze issues that have "depressive or anxious themes," to try and make connections between specific situations and disappointing outcomes. Your wife needs to avoid transferring her disappointment in the gift to the relationship as a whole.

What you need to say and do
Make light of the situation by calling yourself out as a buffoon. Get her to laugh! It will take the pressure off and give everyone a break.

- Apologize for getting it wrong, and then tell her you can't wait to make out with her in the car while listening to the new car stereo.
- Figure out what she really wanted and then surprise her with it a week or two later.

What not to say and do
Don't go overboard with self-criticism. After all, you didn't forget her birthday; you didn't even neglect to get her a present. You just gave her the wrong kind of present. Focus on achieving the best possible outcome, which is to get her to stop feeling bad, cease being angry with you, and convince her that you do pay attention … most of the time.

- Don't over-apologize, but don't get mad at her either.

- Don't over-explain. Just tell her you thought she would like the gift and you're truly sorry she didn't.
- Don't throw more money at the problem. Remember, cost wasn't the issue here.

How both of you will benefit
Tactfully negotiating the fallout of thoughtlessness—whether perceived or actual—is a little-known trick of successful relationships. Remember to treat the situation with levity. Deliver a thoughtful apology and have compassion for your wife's feelings. Finally, be good-humored about the mix-up.

Things to Realize
- Your partner values the intimacy that gift-giving expresses, not the monetary value.
- Your partner wants gifts that are for her—not gifts that are for you or for you both.
- Pay attention to hints, clues, and outright requests for the perfect gift next time.

Invest
as a Team

Women are conservative
investors and are hesitant to
take financial risks.

The Scenario

You wife wants to put a portion of your combined disposable income into savings or CDs, but you want to play the stock market and take advantage of the housing slump to buy an investment property. It seems like a waste of potential wealth to play it so safely, and you are frustrated that she is so opposed to taking a bit of a risk.

Situation at a Glance

- She wants to build a retirement nest egg.
- You want to build riches faster than that.
- She wants to play it safe.
- You want to take a risk.
- She does not want to take the chance of losing any money.
- Your motto is, "You have to play to win."

The problem in this situation

Men and women have fundamentally different investment strategies: men tend to invest aggressively and seek out quick returns. Women are more patient and tend to make conservative, long-term investments. The National Association of Securities Dealers (NASD) learned in the 2006 study "Gender Differences in Investment Behavior" that 51 percent of men will accept "above average" risk when making an investment, compared to just 31 percent of women.

What she really means & what she really needs

Your partner wants to save for her retirement because she wants to protect her future. She's not alone: According to the 2007 Women & Investing Survey conducted by Oppenheimer Funds, Inc., 57 percent of married women focus on retirement as their investment goal. Your wife will be patient with her investments, because she does not want to risk losing any of her retirement funds by moving money in haste.

What you need to say and do

You should incorporate your partner's preferences into your household investment portfolio. After all, you are working with combined finances. In fact, Wall Street Journal columnist Jason Zweig suggested as much in his

May 2009 article, "For Mother's Day, Give Her Reigns to the Portfolio." He said if men included their wives in making important investment decisions, their portfolios would be "less risky and more diversified." Diversifying your portfolio is recommended by financial experts as the wisest way to invest.

- Take your wife's investment ideas seriously.
- Explain your investment strategy to your partner without condescending to her.
- Agree to split your portfolio, assigning half to your investment interests and half to hers. After one year, see which side is doing better and make adjustments.
- See a financial advisor together.

What not to say and do

Don't force your partner to acquiesce to your investment strategy by making her feel less competent or like less of a contributor. However strongly you feel about a particular investment, you should both be onboard. Otherwise, you risk offending, alienating, and marginalizing her.

- Don't make investments behind your partner's back.
- Don't exclude your wife from crucial financial decisions.

- Don't be too stubborn to visit a financial planner, online workshop, or professional strategy session.

How both of you will benefit

Money management is a point of contention in every relationship. But successfully managing the discussion for how to manage your joint finances will relieve a significant amount of tension associated with money talk. Financial harmony is achieved when a couple can talk about money openly, honestly, and without casting aspersions.

Questions to Ask Yourself and Your Partner

- How much of our joint funds are we willing to invest in high-risk, high-yield investments?
- How much money can we afford to contribute to our retirement accounts each month?
- Can we agree on how to diversify our portfolio?
- Should we have separate investments that match our personal strategies?

Tips &
Exercises

Use the following activities,
tips and advice to enhance your discussion
of money and finances.

Money Matters

MarriageEquality.org reports that 43 percent of couples
cited finances as the primary reason they fight. While
some amount of arguing over money is to be expected,
unchecked hostility over your partner's economic
philosophy may lead you straight to divorce court. To
prevent that, work with your partner to establish some
financial ground rules.

Examples include:

- Make a household budget and agree to stick to it.
    - Collect all receipts and track purchases to
      see where spending is in check and where it is
      out of control.

- Make exceptions for special expenses that are important to your partner, and she will do the same for you.

- Schedule monthly meetings to discuss financial concerns.
  - Meet two weeks before most bills are due to decrease last-minute tension.
  - Set time limits for financial discussions and agree to stop talking money when you reach it.
  - Never discuss financial matters in the bedroom.
  - Hold all of your questions/concerns/feedback for the meeting so as not to seem like you are constantly picking on your partner.

- Set financial goals as a team and agree on a plan to reach them.
  - Calculate your combined income and agree on a percentage to use for investing, a percentage for savings, and a percentage to donate to charity.
  - Include "free" money for each of you to spend with no questions asked.
  - Throw all spare change into a piggy bank for your children.

Sex & Intimacy

The HBO series *Sex and the City* depicted sexually active women in a way no other show had ever before—as wholly confident exploring their own sexuality.

It used the 4 female lead characters, Carrie, Charlotte, Miranda, and Samantha, to sift through any and all possible issues women face when they have sex—whether married, in monogamous relationships, or during casual one-night stands. No topic was too raunchy to be considered off-limits. The characters' freedom was a way for female viewers to explore their own sexual fantasies and limitations. It offered a sort of "buffet" of sexual options that women took from the show and fed into their own sex lives.

In the episode, "Easy Come, Easy Go," Samantha, the coital connoisseur, famously quipped, "You men have no idea what we're dealing with down there... Honey, they don't call it a job for nothin'." Hilarious! And true. Women generally feel unappreciated for the effort they put forth to please their partners, and guilty for needing "so much" attention before, during, and after sex.

Figure out why she does what she does:

1. Her libido takes a nosedive whenever she is tired, stressed, or feeling unattractive.

2. She may not feel comfortable trying something new without your encouragement.

3. Sex makes her feel physically and emotionally closer to you.

Whether your partner's sexual personality is that of Charlotte (traditional), Miranda (controlling), Samantha (anything goes), or Carrie (a combination of all of the above) she needs a partner in the bedroom who can keep up with her changing needs. Women are often reluctant to say what they need—make it your job to anticipate these needs. And while women often like their men to take charge and lead the way toward intimacy, they are also more likely to want to be eased into sex. Consider this before groping your partner or outright asking for sex. Men often view sex as a means to end—climax—whereas women view sex as more than just the act; women look forward to the entire journey, from first touch and kiss to orgasm and cuddling.

Above all, make your partner feel as though you get her sexually by treating her body like a racecar—turn it on before speeding to the finish line. Your wife or girlfriend will need different types of intimacy at different stages in your relationship, and proceeding mindfully will help you anticipate these needs.

She's Just Not In the Mood

She doesn't want sex,
but she still wants you.

The Scenario

Your attempts at seducing your wife are often rebuffed because she says she is too tired or not feeling well. You feel like she is rejecting you completely and fear she isn't attracted to you anymore or loves you less than she used too. She maintains she's just not in the mood, but you think that if she loved you she would be attracted to you more often, as you are to her.

Situation at a Glance

- She is rarely in the mood to have sex.
- You are always in the mood for sex.
- She says "no" to sex more often than "yes."
- You wonder if she is still attracted to you.
- She claims she is just busy, tired, or not feeling well.
- You think she is making excuses and feel rejected.

The problem in this situation

Like most men and women, you and your partner have mismatched libidos. Sociology professor Edward O. Laumann, lead author of "The Social Organization of Sexuality: Sexual Practices in the United States," discovered in his research that most men think about sex at least once a day. Only 25 percent of women surveyed thought about sex as often. Men also desire and actively seek out sex much more often than women do—even after years of marriage. In addition, a woman's libido is more negatively affected than a man's by stress, fatigue, and environmental issues, such as a messy house.

What she really means & what she really needs

When your partner says, "I'm not in the mood," she means just that. What she needs depends on the circumstances. She may be too distracted to succumb to your seduction, in which case you should let her be and try again later. Or, she may need more encouragement from you to help kickstart her stalled libido.

What you need to say and do

The times of day your partner least wants sex should be obvious. Examples include when she gets home from work, while she's preparing dinner, after changing diapers, or before she's brushed her teeth in the morning.

Take note of when your partner seems most relaxed and open to your advances, and take advantage of these times. Otherwise, you put her in the position of saying no and set yourself up to feel rejected.

- Know what is going on in your partner's world and use it to your advantage. For example, if she is stressed after work, give her a shoulder or foot massage.
- When you touch her, make it subtle. For example, brush your lips gently across the nape of her neck.
- Set the mood. Clean your bedroom, change the sheets, lay out a nighty for her, light candles, put on her favorite music, and tell her she is about to be spoiled.

What not to say and do
Don't assume she is not attracted to you—instead, examine all possible causes. For example, the birth control pill is a well-known cause of decreased sexual drive in women.

- Don't threaten to get your sexual needs met outside of the marriage.
- Don't accuse your partner of having an affair— unless you have evidence other than her low sex drive.

- Never force sex on your partner.
- Don't hold back from telling your partner that you are wild with desire for her.

How both of you will benefit

Keeping quiet about problems in the bedroom threatens to magnify marital problems. Sex therapist Laura Berman warns that couples who can't discuss their sex life honestly lose empathy for each other, and their "ability to connect is lower." Having honest discussions about sexual expectations increases intimacy, and also challenges you as a couple to get better at meeting each other's needs.

Questions to Ask Your Partner

- What can I do to help you get in the mood to have sex?
- Do you know that I think about making love to you every single day?
- Can you understand that hearing "no" to my attempts to seduce you feels like rejection?
- Is there something intimate that you'd prefer to do?

Make Her Feel Safe

Women have a harder time asking to try new things—be bold and surprise her.

The Scenario

Lately, your partner seems bored during sex. She seems to nudge you here and there but will not just come out and say what she wants you to do. You are reluctant to try new things without knowing if she will be onboard with them, because you don't want her to think you are a pervert or a weirdo.

Situation at a Glance

- She seems to just go through the motions. You think she is bored.
- She wiggles and nudges but never asks for what she wants.
- You want specific instructions on how to please her.
- She wants you to intuit her needs.
- You want to please her, but you're not a mind-reader.

The problem in this situation

Your partner has the romantic idea that you will be able to anticipate her sexual needs. When you don't automatically do what she wants, she tries to help you find your way without saying anything. She pushes your hand here, or moves your mouth there, but you have trouble understanding exactly what she wants. As a result, you both end up frustrated. Her response reads as boredom and you are left confused.

What she really means & what she really needs

Contemporary American women are ostensibly sexually liberated, yet society still teaches girls that talking about sex is "unladylike." Women are trained to be selfless givers and told that correcting a man during sex will insult his manhood. Therefore, most women are not comfortable expressing their needs. In addition, women can become self-conscious about their shifting "sweet spot" and embarrassed about how long it takes to orgasm. Dr. Edward O. Laumann discovered in his survey of sexual practices that it takes men approximately 4 minutes to reach orgasm, whereas it takes women nearly 3 times as long. For all of these reasons, your partner needs you to take charge and become a patient, attentive, and bold lover.

What you need to say and do

Make your partner feel comfortable telling you what she wants. After making love, say something like, "I liked when you were pushing my mouth toward your breasts. I just wasn't sure what you wanted me to do. Can you tell me?" Asking her when the pressure is off increases the likelihood that she will tell you. Once you get a sense for what she wants from you—do it!

- Tell her how much it turns you on when she is on top. It will encourage her to take charge and assure her that you think it is sexy when she is in control.
- Talk dirty during sex. Narrate each touch, taste, and smell as you make love and ask your partner to do the same.
- Create a game out of "tell me what to do," during sex. Take turns giving orders and respond enthusiastically to each of her requests.

What not to say and do

Anything that makes your partner feel self-conscious about her performance will not improve your sex life. Avoid pointing out what you don't like and focus on what you want more of.

- Do not tell her she looks like she is dead, limp, going through the motions, or bored. Instead point out what you like so she does it more often. Say something like, "You look so hot when you move that way, do it again."

- Don't be afraid to take charge and tell her exactly what turns you on in the moment. For example, say "Bend over—I want to take you from behind."
- Don't compare her to your past lovers to get her to compete. It will hurt her feelings and totally backfire.

How both of you will benefit

Coming to a mature, yet hot sex life does not come easily. But every couple can achieve one by having a real conversation about sex. When you stop wondering what your partner needs to be fully engaged during sex, it is as though you've been handed an instruction manual for pleasing her.

Questions to Ask Your Partner

- What is your favorite position when we make love?
- Are you ready to fulfill one of your sexual fantasies?
- Do you want to fulfill one of my fantasies?

Cuddling
Is Worth It

Women need more from sex than just
intercourse—they need connection.

The Scenario

After sex you tend to rush to the bathroom to wash up
and then head to the living room to plop down in front
of the TV. Your partner tells you she wants you to linger
in bed and cuddle with her after sex. You suggest that
she join you on the couch and watch TV. She declines,
clearly disappointed. So you stay in bed, but quickly fall
asleep, which disappoints her too.

Situation at a Glance

- She always seems awake or invigorated after sex.
- You are ready to crash afterwards.
- She is insulted when you rush to the bathroom to
  wash up after sex.
- You don't understand why this bothers her.
- She wants to cuddle in bed, talking and snuggling.

- You don't mind cuddling, but would rather do it while watching TV on the couch.

The problem in this situation

After vaginal and nipple stimulation and orgasm, your partner's body is flooded with the hormone oxytocin. Dubbed the "cuddle hormone" by sexperts, oxytocin—when combined with estrogen—causes your partner to experience a strong desire to bond. Susan Kuchinskas, author of *Love Chemistry: How Oxytocin Lets us Trust, Love and Mate*, notes that although men also experience the calming effects of oxytocin after orgasm, testosterone seems to quell the urge to bond.

What she really means & what she really needs

Most women get lost in the deep emotional connection of sexual intimacy. And once in the post-orgasmic state of relaxation, your partner is ready to begin what is for her the final stage of sex: to cuddle and revel in the glow of connection and release.

What you need to say and do

Your partner is never as relaxed as when she is post-coital. There is no tension, no fighting, no chores, no kids, and nothing else to do in the world but rest together. Think of this time as a mini-vacation from the stressors of your daily life, and enjoy it. Use this time to whisper sweet, affectionate words to hold her against you. You don't have to cuddle for hours, but do give her at least 5 minutes of your full attention after sex.

- She will want to have sex more often if it leads to a place of warm, cuddly bliss. Think of the time spent lingering in bed with your partner after sex as building a bridge toward your next sexual encounter.
- Use the time after sex to tell her things you rarely say, such as "I love you," or "You are a fantastic lover."
- Spoil her after sex by caressing her entire body and planting little kisses on her neck and face.

What not to say and do

According to Ian Kerner, author of *She Comes First*, men return to a "pre-aroused" state after orgasm and experience a "total system shutdown." As a result, you are ready to disengage by falling asleep or watching TV. Of course, you cannot help falling asleep, but don't jump up immediately after orgasm, wash your hands, and announce, "I'm going to watch *The Daily Show*!"

- Avoid curt statements such as, "I'm going to hit the shower now, see you downstairs!"

- Ignore your impulse to move on to the next thing and enjoy what remains of the scent, sweat, and heat from your sexual encounter.
- Don't censor yourself. While you hold her, give a verbal account of what most turned you on while making love.

How both of you will benefit

Making an effort to meet your partner's emotional needs after sex enhances the intimate connection you feel for each other. When you linger after lovemaking for just 5 to 10 minutes of nonsexual contact, you maximize the exchange of emotion.

Things to Realize

- Cuddling can include reading in bed or watching TV together. Just ask her what she prefers before picking up a book or grabbing the remote.
- Hugging, cuddling, and snuggling releases the hormone oxytocin—the same hormone responsible for bonding mother and baby.

Do It Like
the First Time

Foreplay is the most important
component of sex for most women.

The Scenario

When you are turned on, you are immediately ready to
have intercourse. But your partner never seems to match
your level of intensity at the same time, and she always
tries to slow you down with kissing and caressing. You
feel like you are not kids anymore and can skip the coy
petting routine.

Situation at a Glance

- She needs to "warm up" before having intercourse.
- You are ready to go as soon as you have an erection.
- She doesn't like to be rushed.
- You want to get to the good stuff.
- She rarely wants to have a quickie.
- You like foreplay, but don't consider it the
  main event.

The problem in this situation

She needs help getting from her pre-arousal state to feeling lubricated and turned on. Touching, fondling, kissing, and caressing takes time, though—at least 20 minutes. Since all you need is to have an erection and you're ready to go, your pace is quite a bit faster than she can handle.

What she really means & what she really needs

Your partner tries to slow you down before having intercourse because foreplay is her bridge to sex. Foreplay triggers hormones that cause her vagina to become engorged with blood, lubricated, and ready for penetration. She also just likes the way it feels to make out with you. Actress Drew Barrymore put the feelings of millions of women into words when she said, "Kissing, and I mean like, yummy, smacking kissing is the most delicious, most beautiful and passionate thing that two people can do, bar none. Better than sex, hands down."

What you need to say and do

Learn how to read your partner, because she may come to you ready for sex and not require much foreplay at all. Indeed, there will not always be time for 20 minutes of fooling around before intercourse. And in such cases a quickie is called for. She will be more open to these brief encounters if she knows you will give her what she wants the next time.

- Spend at least 5 minutes kissing her. Start with her mouth and work your way down her body.
- Wrap your arms around her from behind. Cup her breasts, lightly pinch her nipples, and run your hands down her torso to tug the waistband of her panties and stop there.
- Let her feel your erection by pressing your body firmly against hers.
- Lie next to her and lightly brush your fingertips from her nose down her body and then let them hover gently over her panties.
- Talk dirty. Whisper what you plan to do to her.

What not to say and do
Foreplay can be a touchy subject for some couples—and not in the physical way. Women often are self-conscious or embarrassed that it takes them "so long" to be ready for sex and then to reach orgasm. As a result they become tense, and everything takes even longer. Your goal is to have her in a relaxed state so that she is open to arousal and responsive to your attempt to seduce her.

- Don't interrupt foreplay to ask, "Are you ever going

to be ready for me?"

- Don't just go through the motions. She will be able to tell if you are not into it.
- Don't embarrass her by saying anything negative about the way she tastes or smells.

How both of you will benefit

Taking time to raise each other's level of passion to unbearable heights will only intensify the orgasms you both enjoy. The longer and more creative the foreplay, the more aroused your partner will get. And don't worry about losing your erection—you will get it back when she turns her attention to you.

Checklist to Gauge Her Level of Arousal

- Her cheeks are flushed and she is breathing heavily.
- Her vagina is wet and engorged and she arches her back.
- She pushes your hand, penis, or mouth toward her vagina.

Tips &
Exercises

Use the following activities, tips and
advice to enhance your sex and intimacy.

Three Steps to a Better Orgasm ... For Her

Avoid using techniques that arouse you on your partner.
She has a separate, unique set of turn-ons, and most of
them require time, patience, and a plot.

Step 1: Create anticipation with a story.
Send her emails or text messages throughout the day with
descriptive snippets of what's to come. Use third person
to give her a voyeuristic experience. For example, write
her something like, "He couldn't stop thinking about
her breasts ... of how when she came home he would
come up behind her, cup them in his hands, and pull her
shirt down past her shoulders."

Step 2: Get her juices flowing.

Women require about 20 minutes of foreplay before they're ready for intercourse. Use this time wisely to get her good and hot. Examples of things you might try include kissing her deeply and passionately; turning down the lights so she feels more relaxed and less self-conscious; teasing her by gently brushing your fingers over her hot spots; and leaving a few items of her clothes on until it's go-time.

Step 3: Don't hold back.

Use a combination of your fingers, tongue, penis, and even toys to increase her pleasure. Alternate digital stimulation with oral sex. Try touching different parts of her vagina and see which she responds most to. Rotate your attention to different parts of her body, and just when things start to get fast, slow them down again. Above all, make her feel like she can take her time to enjoy this pleasurable and loving experience.

Appearance & Health

Comedienne Rita Rudner once joked, "I think men who have a pierced ear are better prepared for marriage. They've experienced pain and bought jewelry." Rudner was commenting on a seemingly universal American reality: that men don't quite get what women go through to look beautiful.

Women spend billions of dollars a year on beauty products and hundreds of hours getting themselves ready to go out. They are constantly updating their wardrobes, shoe collections, and accessories. They spend large portions of their year working out, several hours of their week thinking about food, and thousands of minutes talking about all of the above with their friends. Even with all of the work put into their appearance, women are still engaged in a war against their body image—a war that continues to be perpetrated against women by the television, film, and advertising industries' impossible, yet widely accepted standards of beauty.

By now it is common knowledge that the average American woman bears no resemblance to the average American model, but most people are surprised to find out just how little the two have in common. The average model is 5'11", weighs just 117 pounds, and wears a size

0—the average woman, on the other hand, is 5'4" and wears a size 14. Instead of these dimensions being set as the new standard of beauty, impossibly thin continues to be in.

As a result, women spend a staggering $40 billion a year on dieting and diet-related products, and about half of them admit to trying a fad diet at one point or another. In fact, women are so obsessed with looking good for men that they are even willing to trade their physical well-being for it: A 2009 *Associated Press*/iVillage poll learned that 33 percent of women say they are more concerned with their weight than their physical health.

Figure out why she does what she does:

1. She has internalized society's ideas about beauty.

2. She wants to keep you physically interested in her and prevent you from cheating on her.

3. She believes there is always room for self-improvement.

You play a prominent role in helping your partner overcome her body-image issues. You can even help her dramatically increase her self-esteem, which results in a partner that is more confident, fun, and sexy. One way to effect positive change in your home is to avoid putting pressure on your partner to measure up to an unrealistic beauty ideal. Without supporting laziness, complacency, or overindulgence, love her as she is, and encourage her to be as healthy, strong, confident, and intellectual as you know she is capable of becoming.

Give Her a Dress Break

She needs a break from her usual routine of getting spruced up to go out.

The Scenario

Usually your partner takes great pride in her appearance. But lately, all she wears is sweatsuits and hoodies. Her hair is always up in a ponytail and she rarely wears makeup or perfume. At first you thought it was just a phase, but now you're not so sure. You miss the attractive, smartly dressed person you fell in love with and worry that period of your relationship is over.

Situation at a Glance
- She dresses down when she is at home.
- You think she is letting herself go.
- She says she needs a break from getting ready.
- You miss the way she used to look.
- She says you focus on superficialities.
- You believe how one looks reflects a person's level of happiness, and are concerned about her.

The problem in this situation

She is to the point where she feels safe and comfortable in your relationship, and it shows in her appearance. You, on the other hand, view her sweatsuit as a uniform of complacency. You fear her dressing down indicates the spark has officially gone out. You may find truth in what best-selling author Amy Bloom once wrote: "Love at first sight is easy to understand; it's when two people have been looking at each other for a lifetime that it becomes a miracle."

What she really means & what she really needs

A 2008 Skinbliss survey published in *Marie Claire* magazine discovered that women spend about 65 minutes getting ready every day. In other words, over the course of her lifetime, your partner will spend 3,276 hours—or 136 days—working on her appearance. Less than one-third of the women surveyed actually enjoyed the primping ritual, however, and it seems as though your partner is one of them. She may just need a break from her preen routine.

What you need to say and do

How you respond to her permanent "casual Friday" appearance depends on your relationship. For example, if you usually poke fun at each other, then making jokes about your partner's getup may be acceptable. However, without a jokey, playful foundation, such comments may come across as mean-spirited.

- Reminisce with her about how great she has looked. Say something like, "I was just thinking about how amazing you looked in that red skirt at my sister's party." She will be impressed by your memory and may be inspired to make you see her that way again.
- Plan a night out. Let her know to dress up by sending a text message that says, "You and me tonight. Dress up. Prepare to be dazzled."
- Lead by example. Many women dress down because their husbands put very little effort into their appearance. If you're in workout shorts and a t-shirt all weekend, don't expect her to wear sexy jeans and heels.

What not to say and do

Albert Einstein brilliantly captured the essence of marriage when he wrote, "Women marry men hoping they will change. Men marry women hoping they will not. So each is inevitably disappointed." More than half a century ago, Einstein tapped into the marriage conundrum that you live with every day: how to keep your wife looking like your bride without hurting her feelings?

- Don't tell her you think she is letting herself go.
- When she asks your opinion on something she is considering wearing, don't say, "I don't know" or "I don't care." This makes her think, "Why should I even try?"
- Don't neglect to compliment her when she does make the effort. Women who think their husbands don't notice how they look stop caring about what they wear around them.

How both of you will benefit

Tact is required when it comes to criticizing your partner's appearance. Using positive methods—such as dressing nicely and reminding her of times she dazzled you with her beauty—is the best way to rekindle your partner's desire to dress up.

Checklist for Action
- Buy her a dress and ask her to wear it when you go out.
- Give her reasons to dress up: take her out to dinner, museums, plays, concerts, and other outings.

She's Sexy at Any Size

She is self-deprecating about the weight she's gained and her self-esteem is suffering as a result.

The Scenario

Your wife has yet to lose the last 15 pounds she gained during pregnancy. Whenever she complains that she is "too fat" to fit into her clothes, you say, "So go on a diet! Exercise more!" She gets upset and says "you don't understand how hard it is." You want to support her at any size, but don't understand why she isn't making more of an effort when it makes her so unhappy.

Situation at a Glance

- She still has 15 pounds to lose after giving birth.
- You don't really notice unless she brings it up.
- She constantly talks about her weight.
- You suggest she take action and stop complaining.
- She accuses you of simplifying a serious problem.
- You want to support her, but she shoots down all of your suggestions.

The problem in this situation

The extra weight she carries weighs down more than just her body. Her general happiness is compromised by her inability to drop those final pounds. Even though you love her at any size, she doesn't love herself unless she weighs what she wants to.

What she really means & what she really needs

Count your wife among the more than 50 percent of participants in a 2009 *Associated Press*/iVillage poll who expressed extreme dissatisfaction with their weight. She is also one of the 75 percent of American women who are unhappy with their overall appearance. And with good reason: society's mirror does not reflect kindly on her. She needs you to love her as-is, but she also needs you to be a committed ally in her quest for achieving a healthy weight through good nutrition and exercise.

What you need to say and do

Keep seducing her, compliment her voluptuous curves, and treat her as you did before her weight gain. At the same time, be sensitive to her problem: she wants to lose weight but is having a hard time. Offer to adopt a healthy lifestyle with her so that she doesn't feel alone in her battle of the bulge.

- Plan physical activities for your time together instead of sedentary ones. Go biking, hiking, walking, swimming, or play tennis. Just get off the couch and move together!
- Email your partner low-fat, high-fiber recipes and tell her you'd love to make dinner for her.
- Eat at home more.
- Tell her she looks wonderful, great, cute, adorable, beautiful, sexy, or hot, instead of saying, "You look like you've lost weight!" Placing value on weight loss increases pressure and causes her to focus on the scale.

What not to say and do

When it comes to women and weight, men often feel as though they've wandered onto a mine field. Carefully tread this dangerous issue and avoid these common man-traps:

- Never answer "yes" when she asks, "Does this outfit make me look fat?" Even when she says it's OK to be honest, it's not. What she is actually looking for is affirmation that she looks good in whatever she is wearing.
- Don't try to solve her weight problem for her.
- Don't deny her the chance to talk, complain, cry,

and agonize over how hard it is to lose weight.

How both of you will benefit

When couples get tangled up in society's mixed messages about beauty and happiness, confronting weight issues often takes center stage. Since weight is about lifestyle, you will struggle for a while to redefine the food culture you have created in your relationship. Tackling unhealthy habits as a family and adopting goals that support wellness—instead of focusing on weight— makes achieving good health a top priority and shoves the scale back under the bed.

Things to Realize

- When she feels fat, her self-esteem takes a nose dive.
- Always support her in her weight-loss plan. Never feel threatened by it.
- Don't stock sweets and fatty snacks in your home.
- It can take a year or more for a woman to lose all of the weight she gained during pregnancy.
- If you are sedentary and eat a diet of fast-food, she will find no reason to change her habits; conversely, if you eat well and are active, she will be inspired to do the same.

She Wants You to Live Forever

She cares about what you eat because she cares about you.

The Scenario

You don't eat salads—in fact, the only green thing on your plate is the pickle on your cheeseburger. You drink coffee, soda, juice, or beer, but you don't like the tastelessness of water, so it rarely passes your lips. Your girlfriend is after you to eat better and drink more water, but your philosophy is "live and let live," so you want her to leave you alone.

Situation at a Glance

- You like meat, potatoes, sweets, and anything deep fried.
- She is appalled by your diet.
- You don't get why she cares what you eat. You let her order whatever she wants, why shouldn't she treat you the same?

- She is worried about your health.
- You think she is overreacting.
- She is turned off by your unhealthy habits.

The problem in this situation

Your wife eats meals that follow nutritional experts' advice: she makes her plate look "like a rainbow" of color and includes lots of fresh vegetables, whole grains, and low-fat proteins. You, on the other hand, eat around the green and yellow stuff, and plan your menu according to *Men's Health* magazine's list of Top 20 Worst Foods of 2009.

What she really means & what she really needs

When you were a bachelor your eating habits were your business, but now that you're in a serious, committed relationship, they're up for debate. She nags you about your diet, because she wants to live a long, healthy life—with her. She expects you to take your health seriously because it demonstrates maturity and even a long-term commitment to your relationship. And quite frankly, she is grossed out by your greasy diet.

What you need to say and do

Clinging to a bachelor's diet will not preserve your youth, nor will it establish independence from your partner. So it is time to grow up, change your attitude about food, and choose dishes based on their nutritional value and ability to fuel your body. Indeed, your food choices may literally be a matter of life and death. According to a 2009 National Cancer Institute study, eating just a quarter-pound of red meat per day over 10 years increases a man's risk of dying from cancer by 22 percent and of heart disease by 27 percent.

- Switch to lean fish and chicken and include fresh fruits and vegetables in your diet to decrease your risk.
- Drink 8 to 10 glasses of water daily. It is essential to the functioning of your organs—especially your brain. If you can't stand the taste of water on its own, squeeze fresh lemon or lime into your glass.
- Make a deal with your partner to let you indulge in the foods you like half of the time, and let her meal-plan for you the other half. Work on improving that ratio so that you are only eating greasy, unhealthy foods 10 percent of the time.

What not to say and do
Avoid getting bogged down in a rebellion against your partner's complaints about your diet. Regardless of her delivery, her message is sound: She wants you to be healthy.

- Don't eat red meat more than once a week.
- Avoid eating junk food in front of the TV. If you are hungry make a healthy snack.
- Don't let pride interfere with making healthy choices.
- Don't delude yourself: you are not immune from developing cancer, heart disease, or diabetes.

How both of you will benefit
Adopting a healthy lifestyle as a family makes exercise and eating right feel like a way of life instead of a sacrifice. Besides, couples who eat nutritionally balanced meals and get regular exercise also have increased sex drives and a more satisfying love life.

Things to Realize
- One pound equals 3,500 calories.
- Body Mass Index (BMI) measures body fat based on height and weight: Underweight = <18.5, Normal weight = 18.5-24.9, Overweight = 25-29.9, Obesity = BMI of 30 or greater.

She Needs Her Time to Release

She values physical fitness and cherishes the alone time that her workouts provide.

The Scenario

Your partner goes to the gym almost every day. Even though you think she looks amazing, her gym schedule seems to rule her life. She gets up super early, even on weekends, to get a workout in. You wish she would chill out a little, because her obsession with the gym is starting to interfere with your ability to sleep in or make plans.

Situation at a Glance
- She is dedicated to her workout.
- You think she's going overboard.
- She says she needs to exercise daily or she will be miserable.
- You work out 3 times a week and think that's enough.

- She has to work harder than you do to stay in shape.
- You wonder if she suffers from a serious body image issue.

The problem in this situation

Like most women, your wife is terrified of becoming fat. She can't help it—she was brought up on the message that being fat is weak, unattractive, and a sign of laziness. Consider that teen girls are more afraid of being overweight than they are of nuclear war, cancer, or losing their parents. It is gong to take a lot more than wanting to sleep in to undo your partner's indoctrination in the "thin is in" culture.

What she really means & what she really needs

Your wife worked hard to get to her current level of physical fitness. She clutches her achievement as if her life depended on it—and it just might. Besides the social pressure to remain thin, being overweight significantly increases her risk of death from heart disease, cancer, and diabetes. In addition, she enjoys working out because it is the one time of day to do something that is completely by and for herself.

What you need to say and do

Experts from Stanford University School of Medicine

say there is little to no benefit to working out for more than one hour a day. After that, a person risks injury and fatigue. People that push themselves past their limit several times a week may be addicted to exercise. Share this information with your partner, and also:

- Ask her to set her cell phone to vibrate and use it as her alarm so it doesn't wake you up at 6 a.m. on weekends.
- Let her know you would like to have the option to be spontaneous (with plans, sex, day trips, going out to breakfast, etc.) and ask her to be flexible with when she does her workout.

What not to say and do
Don't try to convince your partner to cut down on her exercise routine. If you even suggest she stop going to the gym—or go less frequently—she may feel like you are trying to control her.

- Don't use guilt as a means to get her to stop going to the gym. For example, don't tell her the kids "wonder if mommy's ever coming home" whenever she goes to the gym. If she really doesn't spend enough time with the children, take that issue up in a separate, straightforward conversation.

- Don't try to limit her time at the gym because you are insecure about your own physical condition. Increase your workouts instead so you can keep up with your woman!

How both of you will benefit
Come up with ways to spend more time together without forcing her to compromise her beloved workouts. Doing so demonstrates that you respect her "me time." Besides, time spent on activities each of you enjoys preserves your individually and keeps the relationship fresh and interesting.

Things to Realize
- She is in great shape because of how often she works out.
- She is not working out to spite you.
- You love her physique.
- Her workout provides deserved time to herself.
- Regular exercise increases sex drive.

Tips &
Exercises

Use the following activities,
tips and advice to enhance your
understanding of appearance and health.

She Wants You to Eat Right and Exercise Because ...

- Men who smoke and are overweight, don't exercise, and eat high-fat, low-fiber diets significantly increase their risk of developing colon cancer.
- Heart disease is the leading cause of death in men. However, just a 10 percent reduction in total cholesterol levels may prevent coronary heart disease by as much as 30 percent.
- Regular exercise decreases stress, releases the feel-good hormone endorphins, and stimulates the libido.

She Wants to Eat Right and Exercise Because ...

- She wants to look and feel her best for you.
- She has been programmed by society to take her appearance and weight very seriously.
- Working out and eating right is something she enjoys doing with and for herself.
- She hopes to live a long, healthy life, and wants you to do the same.

Conclusion

After reading *The Ultimate Guide for Men to Understand Women* you should feel enlightened about some of the confusing interactions you have with your partner. You should understand that your partner is a complex person with conflicting emotions, desires, and expectations that even she sometimes doesn't understand.

With this book at your fingertips, you now have the ability to review applicable scenarios to guide you through the most frustrating arguments and baffling interactions. You should have also gained significant insight into the societal influences that shape your partner's expectations, behavior, and communication style.

In addition, you should feel less like a bystander and more like an active participant in your relationship, because this book has shown you that you are responsible for 50 percent of its successes and failures. By explaining the differences between how men and women demonstrate commitment through their priorities and values—as well as how they communicate about money, sex, and health issues—this book has helped you to understand how to negotiate with your partner in these matters. And by committing to enact the various well-researched suggestions, you have taken your first step toward becoming a better partner. In addition, you now get that trying to understand your partner's needs and desires goes a long way with her, even when you are unable to give her what she wants. Finally, you have learned that the six major components of a relationship require regular maintenance to assure they are all operating at their peak level of performance.

Above all, you should feel confident in the knowledge that your relationship is not a lost cause. In fact, quite the opposite is true. By investing in *The Ultimate Guide for Men to Understand Women*, you have clearly demonstrated a willingness to work diligently at the most precious gift in your life—your relationship.